Looking toward the Cross

A 40-day Easter Journey for Families

ISBN-13: 978-1508429050

Table of Contents

Introduction

Although I grew up going to church, my family did not observe Lent. In fact, it wasn't until I was almost 30 that I realized Catholics are not the only ones who observe the Lenten season.

The word Lent means "spring." The time between winter and summer when the ground thaws and the earth grows green again. It's a time of rebirth leading up to the greatest single event in the history of mankind - the death and resurrection of Jesus the Messiah.

As a protestant who had never once considered pondering Easter as an entire season, I love the idea of Easter being on the horizon for 40 days (the time Jesus spent in the wilderness before starting his ministry) instead of just the week between Palm and Easter Sundays.

Lent is meant to be a solemn season focused solely on the suffering that Jesus took on for us. Some churches don't use their instruments during these six weeks or sing songs of celebration. Most people who observe Lent deny themselves some sort of pleasure during the 40 days. Sundays are considered "Feast Days." Not to be confused with a day for celebration, they are actually set aside to allow the person to partake of whatever they have given up for Lent.

The devotional plan is based around this 6-day format. I also made Saturday optional as families have different schedules on the weekends. The first five Saturdays explain one of the different elements of the observance of Lent: Prayer, Penance, Repentance, Almsgiving, and Self-Denial. The final Saturday of the season is dedicated to a family service project. This also allows those who choose not to touch on the aspects of Lent to skip Saturdays without making a "hole" in their weekday family devotionals.

Each day also lists an activity. These are completely optional. They are for families who have more time in their day to allow for a longer family devotional. The devotionals are written to be able to stand on their own. If you choose, you may skip the activities all together and still focus on Jesus' life and ministry leading up to the crucifixion.

I believe practices such as self-denial during Lent are personal and shouldn't be taken lightly. I believe they shouldn't become ritualistic in nature and hesitate having my children grow up with a practice they haven't chosen for themselves. Although I explain self-denial on the fifth Saturday, it isn't an active part of this devotional. This family book is really just a 40-day devotional written specifically to prepare little hearts for the main event of the resurrection.

I hope you enjoy the journey to the cross as much as we do.

List of Supplies:

Day 1: Crescent rolls or similar, printed verses (printable provided)

Day 2: 8 oz glass of water; blue food coloring

Day 3: Construction paper, Popsicle sticks, glue gun

Day 4: No supplies needed

Day 5: Bleach pen, colored 100% cotton t-shirt, stencil if desired

Day 6: No supplies needed

Day 7: Maze (printable provided)

Day 8: Aluminum Foil or paper;

Day 9: Piece of paper, craft paint, sharpie marker

Day 10: Find a local soup kitchen OR make a batch of chili for a shut-in (recipe not provided)

Day 11: Soft ball, like a tennis ball or plastic ball

Day 12: Flashlight

Day 13: Small pile of sand, flat rock, boxes or bins to contain mess, building blocks

Day 14: White fish fillet (such as halibut, cod, or tilapia) for each person, breadcrumbs, milk, baking dish, oven.

Day 15: No supplies needed

Day 16: Salt, pepper, plate, plastic spoon

Day 17: No supplies needed.

Day 18: Three opaque plastic cups, one small object

Day 19: A dollar bill of any denomination

Day 20: Backpack and books

Day 21: Large Ziploc bags, toothpaste, toothbrush, small soaps (sample size is perfect), washcloth, Bandaids, antibiotic ointment, fingernail clippers, comb/brush, deodorant, small shampoos/conditioners, socks, gloves, and soft snacks such as apple sauce, fruit cups, soft breakfast bars, and chocolate. Don't forget to add a plastic spoon! (have as many of these items as you'd like to make for homeless person care packets)

Day 22: Aluminum can, decorative paper, stickers, markers

Day 23: Water bottles, vinyl lettering or stickers

Day 24: A raw egg

Day 25: Laundry basket, stack of heavy books

Day 26: No supplies needed

Day 27: Salt, water, flour, oven or microwave, rolling pin, mixing bowl, spoon, heart cookie cutter

Day 28: Rice and beans (enough to feed your family)

Day 29: List of 10 Commandments (provided)

Day 30: Construction paper or notebook paper, pen

Day 31: Easter Garden - large tray or large terracotta planter base, soil, 3 small crosses (can be made from twigs or craft sticks) grass seed, small terracotta pot, stone at least 3/4 size of pot opening (refer to picture if necessary)

Day 32: Small empty box gift-wrapped for each child

Day 33: Towel, large plastic bin or water basin, warm water

Day 34: No supplies needed

Day 35: Dinner plate, fresh horseradish, shank bone (or chicken neck), matzot crackers, egg, apple, walnuts, splash of wine, potato, romaine lettuce (or crackers and grape juice for family communion)

Day 36: No supplies needed

Day 37: Several heavy books

Day 38: Two small sticks or craft sticks and twine per person

Day 39: No supplies needed

Day 40: Whole pecans, vinegar, 3 egg whites, salt, sugar, mixing bowl, wooden spoon, Bible, Ziplock baggie, wax paper, cookie sheet, tape, mixer, oven

Day 1 - Ash Wednesday - Jesus in the wilderness

Matthew 4:1-11 Then Jesus was led up by the Spirit into the wilderness to be tempted by the devil. And after He had fasted forty days and forty nights, He then became hungry. And the tempter came and said to Him, "If you are the Son of God, command that these stones become bread." But He answered and said, "It is written, "Man shall not live on bread alone, but on every word that proceeds out of the mouth of God." (Deut. 8:3) Then the devil took Him into the holy city; and he had Him stand on the pinnacle of the temple, and said to Him, "If you are the Son of God throw yourself down for it is written, "He will give his angels charge concerning you" (Ps. 91:11); and "On their hands they will bear you up lest you strike your foot against a stone." (Ps. 91:12) Jesus said to him, "On the other hand it is written, "You shall not put the Lord your God to the test." (Deut. 6:16) Again, the devil took Him to a very high mountain, and showed Him all the kingdoms of the world, and their glory; and he said to Him, "All these things will I give you, if you fall down and worship me." Then Jesus said to him, "Be gone, Satan! For it is written, "You shall worship the Lord your God, and serve Him only." (Deut. 6:13) Then the devil left Him; and

behold, angels came and began to
minister to Him.

Right before starting his ministry, Jesus retreats to the wilderness to pray and fast for 40 days and 40 nights. It says after the 40 days "He became hungry." It was at His weak point that Satan comes to Him and tempts Him. And not only does he tempt Jesus, but he uses scripture to do it - taking it out of context to try and lure Jesus into sinning. Satan is the Father of Lies and sometimes does it by starting with the truth. As we see though, Jesus is well-versed in the scripture and responds with scripture Himself, showing the devil that he cannot use God's word against Jesus.

One of the scriptures Jesus uses is from Deuteronomy 8:3 where Moses is reminding the Israelites about the goodness of what the Lord has done for them bringing them out of Egypt. He tells them that God provided manna from heaven when they were hungry - so much of it that it was a reminder that "man shall not live by bread alone, but by every word that proceeds out of the mouth of God." Food gives us our daily sustenance, but what really sustains our hearts and souls is the Word of God. It's important to learn scripture in its context, how it applies to us and what it tells us about God.

Activity: Print out copies of Deuteronomy 8:3 and cut them into small strips (think fortune cookies). Buy premade crescent roll dough in a can (like Pillsbury). Roll paper into the dough and bake according to package directions. Serve the bread to the children asking them to break it open before eating. You can have the children help you make it or have it ready for an ah-ha moment when they realize scripture is inside.

1. Print and cut out verse. Fold in half twice and place on wide end of dough.

2. Roll into crescent shape and bake according to package directions.

3. When kids open rolls, scripture should be in the middle.

4. Show them that man cannot live only on bread.

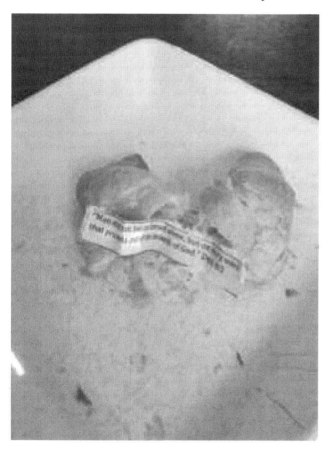

"Man shall not live on bread alone, but on every word that proceeds out of the mouth of God." Deut. 8:3

"Man shall not live on bread alone, but on every word that proceeds out of the mouth of God." Deut. 8:3

"Man shall not live on bread alone, but on every word that proceeds out of the mouth of God." Deut. 8:3

"Man shall not live on bread alone, but on every word that proceeds out of the mouth of God." Deut. 8:3

"Man shall not live on bread alone, but on every word that proceeds out of the mouth of God." Deut. 8:3

"Man shall not live on bread alone, but on every word that proceeds out of the mouth of God." Deut. 8:3

"Man shall not live on bread alone, but on every word that proceeds out of the mouth of God." Deut. 8:3

"Man shall not live on bread alone, but on every word that proceeds out of the mouth of God." Deut. 8:3

Day 2 - Thursday - The Fall

Genesis 3:1-7; 24 Now the serpent was more crafty than any beast of the field which the Lord God had made. And he said to the woman, Indeed, has God said, "You shall not eat from any tree of the garden?" and the woman said to the serpent, "From the fruit of the trees of the garden we may eat; but from the fruit of the tree which is in the middle of the garden, God has said, "You shall not eat from it or touch it, lest you die." And the serpent said to the woman, "You surely shall not die! For God knows that in the day you eat from it your eyes will be opened, and you will be like God, knowing good and evil." When the woman saw that the tree was good for food, and that it was a delight to the eyes, and that the tree was desirable to make one wise, she took from its fruit and ate; and she gave also to her husband with her, and he ate. Then the eyes of both of them were opened and they knew that they were naked; and they sewed fig leaves together and made themselves loin coverings. So He (God) drove man out; and at the east of the Garden of Eden He stationed the cherubim, and the flaming sword which turned every direction, to guard the way to the tree of life.

Long before Satan twisted God's words to tempt Jesus, He successfully convinced Eve into doing exactly what

God had commanded her not to do, dooming us all to have a sinful nature. Romans 5:12 says, "Therefore, just as through one man sin entered into the world, and death through sin, and so death spread to all men, because all sinned --" and Romans 3:23 says, "for all have sinned and fall short of the glory of God."

The sin of the first man and woman brought physical and spiritual death to us all. And unfortunately, Romans 6:23 tells us exactly what God warned in the garden "The wages of sin is death but the free gift of God is eternal life in Christ Jesus our Lord."

Jesus, the Son part of God, came to earth to pay the debt owed for our sins. His death on the cross fulfilled the punishment for everyone's sin and his resurrection defeated death for us.

Activity: Drop a drop of blue food coloring into a glass of water. Watch as it slowly spreads throughout the water. Stir. Talk about how one drop of sin poisoned the whole world.

Day 3 - Friday - Jesus is the Word

John 1:1-5 In the beginning was the
Word, and the Word was with God, and
the Word was God. He was in the
beginning with God. All things came into
being by Him, and apart from Him
nothing came into being that has come
into being. In Him was life, and the life
was the light of men.

John calls Jesus - The Word. Not only was He in the beginning (think Gen. 1:1 - In the beginning....) but He was also present and helped at creation because Jesus is God.... "the Word was with God and the Word was God."

When we think of the scripture, "man shall not live by bread alone" and how Eve so easily questioned the words of God, it reminds us that Jesus is the Word - He is the one who sustains us and guides us.

Activity: Make the name of Jesus with Popsicle Sticks. Parental supervision required. TIPS: I noticed it works better if you use all the same color sticks. Hot glue is very forgiving. If you don't get your sticks together before it dries, peel it off and start again. Also I really had to show my sticks who was boss when cutting them.

1) Using a glue gun, glue two Popsicle sticks into a line by overlapping them end-to-end (do this twice so you have two lines)

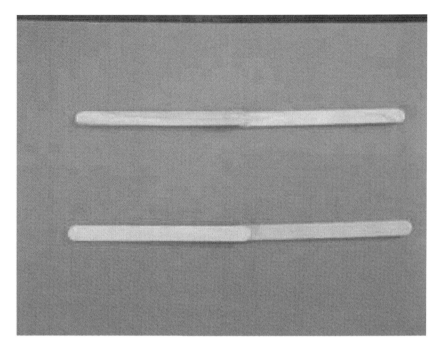

2) Cut three Popsicle sticks in half so you have six equal pieces. Glue them down making sections, starting with one edge and ending with the other. There should be five total sections when you're done. The first section can be a little narrower than the other four. (One section for each letter in the name Jesus.)

3) Cut 4 more Popsicle sticks into pieces as demonstrated below.

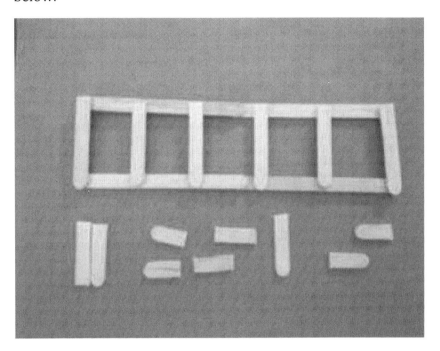

4) Glue smaller pieces as demonstrated below to form the name Jesus in the "white" space.

Ask children what word they see... JESUS is the word!

Day 4 - First Saturday of Lent - Prayer

Romans 5:8 God demonstrates His love
toward us in that while we were yet
sinners Christ died for us.

It's easy to be nice to someone acting kind toward us. God loved us even before we were "nice" to Him. Isn't it amazing that God looks at us in our sinful, imperfect state and loves us no matter what? There's nothing we can do to cause God to love us more, and there's nothing we can do to cause God to love us less. He simply loves us. Oh how He loves us!

The first way we prepare our hearts during Lent is by focused prayer. Paul calls us to a life of praying without ceasing (I Thessalonians 5:17) so Lent isn't the only time we pray. Lent is a time to come before the God of Creation focusing on what He has done for us through His Son's death on the Cross. This is not necessarily a time of praying and fasting for a burden we carry on earth (for example, the salvation of family members, the healing of a loved one). It is one of focusing on what Jesus did for us on the cross. For our purposes you may choose any topic you wish to pray for during this 40-day journey.

Activity: Focus on the prayer of Lent. Take time as a family to thank God for who He is, for sending His Son to the earth, and for loving us so unconditionally. Confess (either silently or aloud) those things that keep us from relationship with Him. This is not a time to bring up old sins that you've already asked forgiveness for... this is a time to have true repentance for on-going sins or to acknowledge that we are all sinners and in need of salvation through the blood of Christ.

2 Chronicles 7:14 If my people, who are called by my name, will humble themselves and pray and seek my face and turn from their wicked ways, then I will hear from heaven, and I will forgive their sin and will heal their land.

Optional activity: You may also choose to pray for something specific as a family for the next 36 days, for example, the poor around the world, the persecuted church, those exploited by human trafficking, orphans, and so on.... the topics are endless! Write the prayer requests in a journal that you can update each week.

First Sunday of Lent -

Sundays are a timeout from the self-denial aspect of Lent. This is a day one may partake in gratitude of Christ's sacrifice. Although it is considered a "Feast Day" as opposed to a "Fast/Abstaining Day", it still calls for a time of reflection and solemnity. If you have chosen not to focus on self-denial during this journey, this is an extra day to discuss what you are learning as a family.

At lunch, talk about what you each learned in church this week. End with a family prayer - it doesn't have to be long... just a time to pray for the things you decided to focus on during yesterday's devotional. If you chose not to do Saturday's devotional, take a moment to choose one (or more) prayer requests to focus on for the next 36 days as a family.

Day 5 - Monday - The Lamb of God

John 1:29 The next day he (John the Baptist) saw Jesus coming to him and he said, "Behold, the Lamb of God who takes away the sin of the world!"

To understand the significance of Jesus being the Lamb of God, we must go back to the Israelites' time in Egypt. They were slaves for hundreds of years after Joseph and the Pharaoh died. The new Pharaoh saw how many children they were having. He was afraid they would take over the nation of Egypt and take his power away so he forced them into slavery. God allowed them to be slaves for several generations before sending Moses to deliver them from Egypt.

However, Pharaoh's heart was hardened and he would not let the people go. God sent a series of 10 plagues. The tenth and final one was an Angel of Death who came through the land and took the life of the oldest child in every household. The ONLY way to save your child was to kill a lamb and paint your doorframe with its blood. The memorial of this event is called Passover. Pretty gruesome, but the blood of the lamb was salvation for many Hebrew children that night and the absence of it was the death of every oldest Egyptian child, including the eldest son of the Pharaoh. This heartbreak is what made the Pharaoh finally let the children of Israel go.

The symbol of the lamb's blood as a sacrifice or an instrument of salvation is woven all throughout the story of the Israelite people. There were special church ceremonies they had to perform at certain times of the year to make themselves acceptable to God involving the blood of a spotless lamb. When John the Baptist called Jesus the Lamb of God it was a huge, cultural sign that the Messiah had come. In that phrase he was signifying that Jesus would be the final payment for the sins of the Jewish people (and all the world). There would be no more need for sacrificing lambs - Jesus is The Lamb - and He took away the sins of the world.

Activity: Make a bleach pen t-shirt

1. Take a colored t-shirt. (I put a piece of cardboard in between the front and back of the shirt so bleach didn't bleed through.

2. Have kids use a bleach pen to make a design on the t-shirt. (You can use a stencil if you wish. If making multiple designs from stencil, wash and dry between uses.) Explain that the bleach removes the color from the shirt just like Jesus removes our sin. Your design can be simple or intricate depending on age.

3. Let the bleach dry to desired color or all the way to white. (up to 3 hrs)

4. Rinse in cold water to remove any remaining bleach.

5. Wash with like colors and dry.

6. Proudly wear the shirt and remember that Jesus, the Lamb, takes away our sins.

Optional scripture reading - the Baptism of Jesus, (Matt. 3:13-17) the Exodus from Egypt (Exodus chapters 1-14)

Day 6 - Tuesday - Jesus starts his ministry

Matthew 4:17 From that time Jesus began
to preach and say, "Repent for the
kingdom of heaven is at hand."

Jesus starts his ministry at the core of the issue. To be in a right relationship with God, we must recognize we are sinners and turn our hearts from ourselves and toward Christ. Repentance indicates an actual change of mind... a willful act of leaving our past behavior behind us. Our natural instinct is to think only of ourselves and our own needs. Repentance brings us to a place where we think of Christ and His will for our lives.

The gospel is simple: Sin separates us from God. We are sinners. The only way to a right relationship with God is through the sacrifice of Jesus Christ; and to accept the gift of life, we must confess our sins and turn from them (repentance). Ask God to help you do that today.

Activity: The "Repentance" Game. Stand with your children directly in front of you, but facing away from you. When you shout, "Run!" they should run as fast as they can away from you. When you shout, "Turn" they should turn around and run back toward you. Repeat. Talk about how when we aren't willing to repent of our sins, we are running away from God, but when we repent, we *must* turn away from our sinful ways and run toward Him.

Day 7 - Wednesday - Jesus is the way, the truth, and the life

John 14:6 Jesus said to him, "I am the way, and the truth, and the life; no one comes to the Father, but through me."

Yesterday we talked about the first step to a relationship with God - understanding we are sinners and coming to repentance. Today we see the second step - understanding that forgiveness for our sins comes through the blood of Christ. This is what John the Baptist meant by Jesus being the Lamb of God. There is no other way to approach God, except through his son.

It may seem arrogant at first glance to think the ONLY way to heaven is through Jesus. But when we remember that He is part of God, we realize God is saying, "the way to come to me is through me."

Activity: Complete the maze on the following page. Talk about how there is only one way from the beginning to end and turning off the path takes you to a dead end.

start

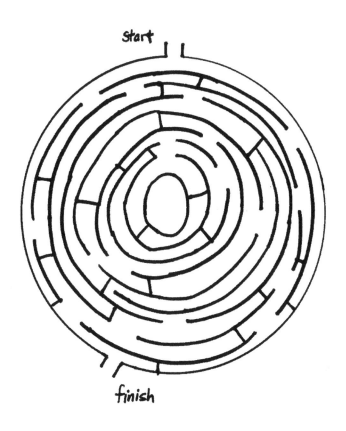

finish

Day 8 - Thursday - Jesus calms the storm

Matthew 8: 23-27 And when He (Jesus)
got into the boat, His disciples followed
Him. And behold, there arose a great
storm in the sea, so that the boat was
covered with the waves; but He Himself
was asleep. And they came to Him, and
awoke Him, saying, "Save us, Lord; we are
perishing!" And He said to them, "Why are
you afraid, you men of little faith?" Then
He arose, and rebuked the winds and the
sea; and it became perfectly calm. And the
men marveled saying, "What kind of a
man is this, that even the winds and the
sea obey Him?"

You may have never been in a boat during a dangerous
storm, but at some time in your life you will encounter
a trouble so big you know you can't handle it on your own.
Jesus asks us, "Why are you afraid?" Essentially, "Do you
trust me?"

This passage is such a great real-life example of what
salvation is. The disciples say, "Save us Lord; we are
perishing!" And we are! Without Christ we will live an
eternity of literal agony. But when we look to Jesus and put
our faith in Him, death cannot defeat us. (John 3:16) When
you are confused and afraid, cry out to Jesus!

Activity: Make a boat from aluminum foil or paper:

Step 1: Take a plain piece of paper, fold in half

2.Fold in half again like you're making a card. Open your
"card" up and fold down corners to make perfect triangles

on each side of the crease, meeting in the middle (much like making a paper airplane.) There will be a little margin of paper left at the bottom of your triangles.

3. Fold one side of the bottom up over the triangles and then the other, like a paper hat.

4. You will have two small overhangs from the bottom, fold over each corner, one section, then the other, to make a perfect triangle.

5. Fold the triangle tip one way then the other, creating a crease.

6. Open up your triangle and keep opening until it collapses into a square.

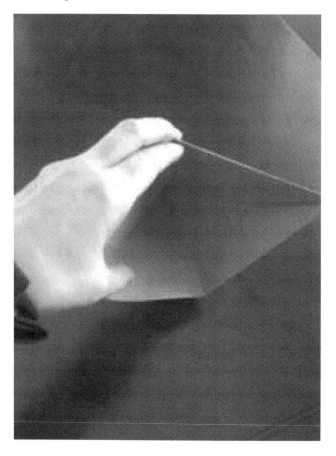

7. Fold the bottom of each side upward to make a triangle. Then bring back down. You're creating a crease. Once you have your creases, you should be able to set the paper on the table with triangle coming off a square base by opening the two bottom sections and leaving the top two together.

8. This is where you kindof have to man-handle your paper to make it into a boat. Widen the bottom section while pushing in on the sides of the top section. You want to make a little rim around your hat triangle to keep the water out.

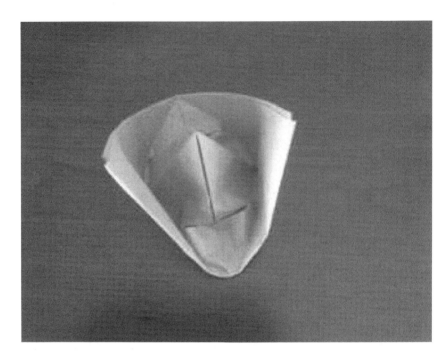

9. The paper absorbs the water a little so will only float for a little while. While paper is easier not to rip, aluminum foil will float longer. Have fun!

Day 9 - Friday - Jesus calms His people

Philippians 4:6-7 Do not worry for anything. But pray and ask God for everything you need. And when you pray, always give thanks. And God's peace will keep your hearts and minds in Christ Jesus. The peace that God gives is so great that we cannot understand it.

Yesterday we saw that Jesus calmed the storm and peace came over the disciples because they saw the strength of their master. Over and over Christ tells us He is good. He is trustworthy. It is because of this that when our circumstances don't change we can trust that Jesus is in control. Paul tells the Philippians not to worry for anything. He gives specific steps to feeling the peace of God. It starts with praying... peace from God ALWAYS starts by talking to him. Praying doesn't have to be a long, drawn out process. It can be as little as one word or thought directed to heaven.

Peace also comes from asking God for what we need. He knows what we need, but there is something about asking Him for help that enables us to give our burdens over to Him.

The third thing we should do is give thanks for things He's already done for us. This helps us remember how faithful and good He is. It reminds us of what He's done for us in the past. It's like taking a big, calming breath and saying, "I know you've got this, because you've proven yourself before."

And then the interesting thing... the verse doesn't say our circumstances will change (like it did for the disciples in the storm), it says the *peace* of God will fill our hearts and minds. There's the miracle, kids! We can have peace while the "storm" rages because we hand it over to the master. It says the peace is so strong that it's hard for us to understand how we can have it in the midst of our trials.

Activity: Make a thankful handprint.

1. Spread paint on each person's hand. Make sure you have a good amount. (I used a sponge brush to spread paint)

2. Lay hand flat on a piece of plain paper.

3. Once dry, write with a sharpie marker one thing you are thankful for on each finger. Have kids think outside the box by listing things that don't include family or material goods. Some examples are weather from that day, hot water, indoor plumbing, a smile from a friend, a hug when we need it, etc. Explain that being thankful for things God has already done, helps us trust Him to supply for our future.

Day 10 - Second Saturday of Lent - Penance

1 John 1:9 If we confess our sins He is
faithful and just to forgive us of all
unrighteousness.

The second way we prepare out hearts during Lent is through Penance. Penance is the act of doing something to "make up for" a sin you've committed. It's important to understand forgiveness comes through confession before God and not through penance. Confession brings one back into a right standing before God whereas penance reminds one not to sin again.

Any penance done throughout this journey should point toward the gospel and what Jesus asks of us as followers of Christ.

Penance Activity: Volunteer as a family at a local soup kitchen. If your children are too young, have them help you make a big pot of chili or soup to take to a shut-in.

Second Sunday of Lent:

At lunch, talk about what you each learned in church this week. End with a family prayer - it doesn't have to be long... just a time to pray for the things you decided to focus on during the forty-day journey.

Day 11 - Monday - Jesus walks on water

Matthew 14:22-32 And immediately He made the disciples get into the boat, and go ahead of Him to the other side, while He sent the multitudes away. And after He had sent the multitudes away, He went up to the mountain by Himself to pray; and when it was evening, He was there alone. But the boat was already many stadia away from the land, battered by the waves; for the wind was contrary. And in the fourth watch of the night He came to them, walking on the sea. And when the disciples saw Him walking on the sea, they were frightened, saying, "It is a ghost!" And they cried out for fear. But immediately Jesus spoke to them saying, "Take courage, it is I; do not be afraid." And Peter answered Him and said, "Lord, if it is You, command me to come to You on the water." And He said, "Come!" And Peter got out of the boat, and walked on the water and came toward Jesus. But seeing the wind, he became afraid, and beginning to sink, he cried out, saying, "Lord, save me!" And immediately Jesus stretched out His hand and took hold of him, and said to him, "O you of little faith, why did you doubt?" And when they got into the boat, the wind stopped.

When we keep our eyes fixed on Jesus we are able to withstand the storm and do powerful things. When we start to focus on our worries and take our eyes off Him, life overwhelms us and we start to sink. What I love is that when Peter cried out for help, it says Jesus immediately reached out for him. He didn't chastise him first, or make him wait longer to learn a deeper message. He responded immediately. He is there to do the same for us when we call on His name.

Activity: Ball Toss

1. Have child stand opposite of you.

2. Toss her the ball gently so she can catch it. Explain that the way to successfully catch the ball is by keeping an eye on it.

3. Have the child close her eyes or look to the side.

4. Throw the ball again. (she will inevitably not catch it) Explain that when we take our eyes off the ball it's harder to catch, just like when we take our eyes off Jesus our problems get harder.

Day 12 - Tuesday - Jesus is the light of the world

John 8:12 Again therefore Jesus spoke to them saying, "I am the light of the world; he who follows me shall not walk in darkness but shall have the light of life."

Psalm 119:105 Thy word is a lamp unto my feet and a light unto my path.

Proverbs 4:19 "But the path of the wicked is like a dark night. They trip and fall over what they cannot see."

Have you ever tripped over something walking around in the dark at night? Or stubbed your toe? That's the worst! The Bible tells us that those who don't believe in Christ live in darkness. They stumble around in life wondering why they keep tripping over things. Christ tells us in John 8 that He is the light of the world. He lights up our darkest night to show us the way to eternal life. Does this mean we will have carefree days? Or never mess up, or never make poor decisions? Certainly not! But it does tell us that Christ and God's word opens our eyes to living a life with Him - one that truly satisfies in a world that so often leaves us disappointed.

Activity: Flashlight illumination 1. Go as a group into a dark room like a bathroom or a closet. 2. Turn off all the lights so it's pitch black. Explain how walking around without God's light is like walking around in a dark room. Turn the flashlight on. Explain how God's spirit in us lights our way.

Day 13 - Wednesday - What is our foundation?

> Luke 6:46-49 And why do you call Me, Lord, Lord and do not do what I say? Everyone who comes to me and hears My words, and acts upon them, I will show you whom he is like: he is like a man building a house, who dug deep and laid a foundation up on the rock; and when a flood rose, the torrent burst against that house and could not shake it, because it had been well built. But the one who has heard and has not acted accordingly is like a man who built a house upon the ground without any foundation; and the torrent burst against it and immediately it collapsed, and the ruin of that house was great.

God gives us His word to help protect us from sin's destruction. He doesn't give us commandments so we don't have fun in life or to make us social outcasts. Those who ignore the wisdom of the Word of God eventually find themselves on shaky ground paying the consequences for their ungodly decisions and actions. When life gets hard, a life built on something other than the Word of God falls down.

Activity: Place a good-sized flat rock inside a small plastic sorting bin. Build a simple structure with wooden blocks on the rock;

Place a small pile of sand in a plastic sorting bin then build a simple structure with wooden blocks on the pile of sand. (this should be a loose pile of sand).

Pour enough water into the basin that it displaces the sand, or comes almost to the top of the rock. The water should not touch the blocks. Which one is more stable? (the displaced sand should spread into the rest of the basin and the block tower should fall, if it stood up in the first place.)

Day 14 - Thursday - Feeding the 5,000

Matthew 14: 14-21 And when He went ashore, He saw a great multitude, and felt compassion for them, and healed their sick. And when it was evening, the disciples came to Him, saying, "The place is desolate, and the time is already past; so send the multitudes away, that they may go into the villages and buy food for themselves." But Jesus said to them, "They do not need to go away; you give them something to eat!" And they said to Him, "We have here only fives loaves and two fish." And He said, "Bring them here to Me." And ordering the multitudes to recline on the grass, He took the five loaves and the two fish, and looking up toward heaven, He blessed the food, and breaking the loaves He gave them to the disciples, and the disciples gave to the multitudes, and they all ate, and were satisfied. And they picked up what was left over of the broken pieces, twelve full baskets. And there were about 5,000 men who ate, aside from women and children.

If you knew there was a great magician in town, would you want to go meet him? How about someone who was so wise He could answer all your questions? Many people wanted to see Jesus. They had heard He was a great teacher and miracle worker. Miracles are better than magic because they aren't just tricks... they change something forever. Jesus' miracles were things like making a storm stop, healing a sick boy, or making a blind man see. When Jesus came to a new town, people gathered to see what He would do next.

On this day, He was so busy teaching them and healing their sick that many hours passed and it was dinnertime. The people were hungry and thirsty, but they'd followed Jesus to a place outside of town where there was no food. When the disciples tell Jesus it's time to send the people away, He doesn't want to stop. Instead He does another miracle. He takes just five loaves of bread and two fishes and starts breaking off pieces to feed the people. Instead of running out, the disciples give out food to over 5,000 people. And not just a bite here and there, but enough so they weren't hungry anymore. In the end, the disciples have twelve baskets of food left over, all from just a handful of ingredients to start.

Activity: Bake homemade fish sticks!

1. Take any white fish fillet and cut into strips

2. Pour about a cup of milk in a shallow dish. In a separate dish, pour about a cup of breadcrumbs.

2. Dunk fish strip in milk to thoroughly coat it.

3. Lay strip in breadcrumbs and flip, coating each side.

4. Place on baking sheet

5. Bake at 350 degrees F for 10 minutes or until cooked through depending on thickness. (center will be opaque and fish will easily flake apart with a fork.)

Day 15 - Friday - Jesus as Truth

John 8: 31-32 Jesus therefore was saying to those Jews who had believed Him, "If you abide in My word then you are truly disciples of Mine, and you shall know the truth, and the truth shall make you free."

Jesus is talking to believers - Jewish ones in the passage - but to us as well if we believe He is the Savior. He tells them that those who follow His words (and the Word of God) are His disciples. He tells them by following His word we know the truth and that truth sets us free.

What does He mean, "Know the truth?" Jesus answers that in John 14:6 "I am the way, **and the truth**, and the life..." JESUS is The Truth that sets us free. There's no way to be free from the power of sin without first turning to the One who takes away our sin. He makes it possible for us to live a life pleasing to God. We can try to "be good" on our own, but knowing Him is what sets us free. Focusing on being good without knowing the One who is good (Ps. 136:1; Ps. 100:5) doesn't help us in the long run. We can't be good for the long-term on our own. Knowing Christ should be our focus. A good start is reading and memorizing God's Word (the Bible) and praying. The more we spend time with God, the more we get to know Him and the Truth (His Son), the more we find ourselves wanting to do what's right.

We know this because Jesus says further down in the passage (vs. 34, 36) "Everyone who commits sin is the slave of sin... If therefore the Son (Jesus) shall make you free, you shall be free indeed." Knowing Jesus is the key to freedom.

Activity: Memorize John 14:6 "I am the way, and the truth, and the life. No man comes to the Father, but through me."

Day 16 - Third Saturday of Lent - Repentance

Repentance isn't to be confused with simply being sorry. Repentance is recognizing our sinful behavior, being sad over it, and then changing our future behavior because of it. John Piper, a Christian pastor and author describes repentance for salvation as "experiencing a change of mind that now sees God as true and beautiful and worthy of all our praise and all our obedience."

Think about that... our view of God is what causes us to repent. When we understand what an eternity in hell means for us, and the fact that Jesus came to earth to save us from that, we cannot help but fall to our knees in worship; and we can't help but want to live a life devoted to God. When we repent and ask Jesus to forgive us of our sins, they are removed from us so that when God looks at us, He sees the perfect righteousness given to us by Jesus.

Repentance Activity:

1. Set out a colored plate.

2. Sprinkle a good-sized pile of table salt onto the plate. Explain to the children that our hearts need to be pure before God.

3. Put a pinch of black pepper on top of the salt. Explain that sin in our lives leaves its mark.

4. Take a plastic spoon that you've rubbed on your clothing (or your hair if necessary!) and run it along the top of the salt and pepper. The pepper should gravitate to it and leave the salt nice and white again.

5. Explain how the death and resurrection of Jesus puts us in a right relationship with God and how this can only happen if we repent.

Third Sunday of Lent:

At lunch, talk about what you each learned in church this week. End with a family prayer - it doesn't have to be long... just a time to pray for the things you decided to focus on during the forty-day journey.

Day 17 - Monday - Jesus as shepherd

John 10: 27-28 My sheep hear My voice
and I know them, and they follow Me; and
I give eternal life to them, and they shall
never perish; and no one shall snatch
them out of my hand.

A shepherd is someone who cares for sheep. He guides, provides, and protects. His job is to lead the sheep to good grass where they can get enough to eat, take them to fresh water to get enough to drink, and protect them from wild animals that want to kill and eat them. Jesus is our shepherd. He guides us with his word, provides for all our needs, and protects us from the devil (1 Peter 5:8). Sheep know their shepherd's voice because they spend so much time with him. The more time you spend getting to know God through the Bible and prayer, the more you will be able to recognize His voice in your life.

Activity: Play a version of Marco Polo where the "blind" person has to catch people in the family in a certain order. They will only know them by their voice.

Day 18 - Tuesday - The one and 99 (The Good Shepherd)

Luke 15:3-7 And He told them this parable saying, "What man among you, if he has a hundred sheep and has lost one of them, does not leave the ninety-nine in the open pasture, and go after the one which is lost, until he finds it? And when he has found it, he lays it on his shoulders, rejoicing. And when he comes home, he calls together his friends and his neighbors, saying to them, 'Rejoice with me, for I have found my sheep which was lost.' I tell you that in the same way, there will be more joy in heaven over one sinner who repents, than over ninety-nine righteous persons who need no repentance."

Sometimes when a flock of sheep is out grazing, one of the sheep wanders away from the group. They have poor depth perception so often fall into ditches or ravines. Part of the shepherd's job is rescuing these lost sheep. Jesus again compares Himself to a shepherd looking for lost "sheep." We are those sheep! God cares for each lost person. He sees each one of us as individuals that He wants to save. He says that He would leave the 99 sheep that aren't lost to go looking for the one who is. We aren't just a number to God.

Activity: The Lost Lamb game - Take three opaque plastic cups and place them open-side down on the table. Put a small object (even better if it's a lamb) under one of the cups. Rotate them quickly over the surface of the table. See if kids can keep track of where the "lost lamb" is.

Day 19 - Wednesday - God is Love

John 3:16 For God loved the world so
much that He gave His one and only Son,
so that everyone who believes in Him will
not perish but have eternal life. (New
Living Translation)

God loves us. Not because we are perfect or for anything that we can do for Him. He loves us because we are His creation. His children. Sin got in the way of Him being with us and because of that Jesus came to earth to die on the cross to get rid of our sins. The way we get that forgiveness is by believing that Jesus is the only way for us to get into a relationship with God. It's hard to imagine the kind of love that dies for the person it loves, but that is how big God's love for us is.

Activity: Take a dollar bill (the higher the denomination the better). Hold it up and ask the kids if they want it. Crumple it up, stomp on it, fold the corners down. Make it as undesirable looking as possible.

Ask again.... who wants this?

Explain that no matter what we've done, God still loves us and finds value in us because we are His creation. There's nothing we can do to make God love us more and there's nothing we can do to make God love us less. No matter what we've done, Jesus still came to earth to die for our sins. We can find forgiveness and peace when we accept Jesus as our Savior. And it's all because of God's love.

Day 20 - Thursday - Jesus will give you rest!

Matthew 11:28-30 Come to Me, all who
are weary and heavy-laden, and I will give
you rest. Take My yoke upon you, and
learn from Me, for I am gentle and humble
in heart; and you shall find rest for our
souls, for My yoke is easy and my load is
light.

People used to use animals to carry things for them on long journeys and to plow their fields to plant seeds. A yoke hooks animals together to work as teams. They were very large and made of heavy pieces of wood.

The weight of the law given to the Israelites was heavy. There were many rules they had to remember and keep perfectly. There were many ceremonies and traditions they had to perform each year with the priests to make themselves clean (or acceptable) before God.

When Jesus died on the cross, He changed all that. His death satisfies God FOR us (Matthew 5:17). This means when God looks at us, if we believe on Jesus Christ, He sees the perfection of Jesus and not our sins (1John 2:2). This is why Jesus says, "Come to me... my burden is light." In other words, when we believe on Jesus, we no longer are required to be perfect to get into heaven (something that's impossible anyway). We are only required to believe on Him - and when we do, we naturally are tempted to sin less and less as we realize all that He's done for us.

Activity: Place a reasonable amount of books inside a backpack. Have each child take turns putting it on their back and doing a lap around the first floor of your home, running a certain distance, or going up and down a flight of stairs. The idea is to get them to understand the weight of carrying around something we can take off....

Have them take it off and perform the activity again. Explain that Jesus wants to take our burdens from us, including our sin. He wants to carry the backpack for us. When we feel weighed down by life, we can pray and tell God we want Him to carry the weight for us.

Day 21 - Friday - God is in the little things

Matthew 15: 32 And Jesus called His
disciples to Him, and said, "I feel
compassion for the multitude, because
they have remained with Me now three
days and have nothing to eat; and I do not
wish to send them away hungry, lest they
faint on the way."

When Jesus spoke to His disciples in this verse, He had been out with the same crowd for three whole days, healing their sick, making lame people walk, and causing the blind to see. He performed many miracles in those three days and was probably pretty tired. It was time to send the people away. He needed rest. But He looked around at their needs - not just their spiritual needs, or their "big" needs for healing, but their practical need for food. He felt compassion for them. So He sets about providing for their most basic needs. The following verses describe Him feeding over 4,000 people, this time with seven loaves of bread and a few fish.

Sometimes we think we should only go to God with the big stuff... with the stuff that is life or death, or only spiritual in nature. These verses show us that God is in the practical details of our lives as well. These people weren't poor, without the means to go home and get food on their own. He wasn't worried that they didn't know where their next meal was coming from. He was more concerned that they needed food now and didn't want to send them away hungry. When you are facing a situation that overwhelms you - even if it seems insignificant and small compared to what others face... maybe you think it's not as important as the starving people in Africa or someone who is facing a serious illness - take it to God anyway. He's waiting for us to rely on him for *every day things*... for us to have faith that He cares for us in big and small ways.

Activity: Homeless Packets

In a large Ziploc bag, place toothpaste, toothbrush, small soaps (sample size is perfect), washcloth, Band-aids, antibiotic ointment, fingernail clippers, comb/brush, deodorant, small shampoos/conditioners, socks, gloves, and soft snacks such as apple sauce, fruit cups, soft breakfast bars, and chocolate. Don't forget to add a plastic spoon!

Make up a few of these and either deliver them, or stick them in your glove compartment for when you see a homeless person. Explain to the children that God provides for our every day practical needs and many times He does this through other people.

Day 22 - Fourth Saturday of Lent - Almsgiving

James 1:27 This is pure and undefiled
religion in the sight of our God and
Father, to visit orphans and widows in
their distress, and to keep oneself
unstained by the world.

Isaiah 58:10 And if you give yourself to
the hungry, and satisfy the desire of the
afflicted, Then your light will rise in
darkness and your gloom will become like
midday.

By definition, almsgiving is doing something kind for another person without expectation of getting something in return, and in most cases it's done for someone less fortunate than the giver. Most people think of almsgiving as giving money, but it can come in many forms. A few examples are giving of your time to help someone out (tutoring, childcare, lawn services, etc) or giving items they need (like a coat drive, or food to a food bank). Be careful of your motives. Jesus warns us in Matthew that we shouldn't do good things so others think highly of us. We must be careful that our motive in doing good comes out of the love Christ has shown us (Matt. 6:1-4).

Almsgiving Activity: Set up a change jar in the kitchen. Put spare change in it at the end of each day. When it's full, donate it anonymously to a local charity. Let the kids decorate the jar to be something meaningful and fun.

With older children: Take some time to plan a service project that you can complete on the sixth Saturday of our 40-day journey. This will be the Saturday before Palm

Sunday. There are plenty of needs in your local community and around the world. Here are some ideas to get you started: volunteer at a local children's hospital to hold babies or play with children while the parents take a break; sing hymns at an nursing home; take a meal to a shut-in from your church and sit and talk awhile; take bag lunches to homeless people on your local streets (make sure the food is soft as many of them don't have all their teeth); do a fundraising campaign to raise money for a well in an impoverished area overseas as a symbol of the Living Water we find in Christ. You can do this through organizations like World Vision or Charity Water.)

Fourth Sunday of Lent:

At lunch, talk about what you each learned in church this week. End with a family prayer - it doesn't have to be long... just a time to pray for the things you decided to focus on during the forty-day journey.

Day 23 - Monday - The woman at the well

John 4:7-14 There came a woman of Samaria to draw water. Jesus said to her, "Give me a drink." For His disciples had gone away into the city to buy food. The Samaritan woman therefore said to Him, "How is it that you, being a Jew, ask me for a drink since I am a Samaritan woman?" (For Jews have no dealings with Samaritans.) Jesus answered and said to her, "If you knew the gift of God and who it is who says to you, 'Give me a drink,' you would have asked him, and he would have given you living water." She said to Him, "Sir you have nothing to draw with and the well is deep; where then do you get that living water?" You are not greater than our father Jacob, are you, who gave us the well, and drank of it himself, and his sons, and his cattle?" Jesus answered and said to her, "Everyone who drinks of this water shall thirst again; but whoever drinks of the water that I shall give him shall never thirst; but the water that I shall give him shall become in him a well of water springing up to eternal life."

Jesus asks the Samaritan woman for a drink, but quickly changes the conversation from his physical needs to her spiritual ones. He tells her that anyone who drinks the Living Water He offers will never thirst again.

You see, God made us to desire a relationship with Him. Deep down we long for true intimacy with our creator but many people feel that longing and try to fill it with things the world has to offer. There are many things that give us pleasure and make us feel good for a little bit - eating delicious food, playing games, watching fun movies. These things are not necessarily bad, but they will never fill that God-sized hole in our hearts. The only thing that will give us a deep, down satisfaction is a relationship with the one true God.

When you are feeling hopeless, restless, or discouraged it's easy to try and reach for something here on earth to make you feel better. Instead take it to God and talk to him about it.

Activity: Personalize water bottles with stickers or vinyl letters. I got my water bottles from the Dollar Store (BPA free!) and used some stickers we had around the house.

Day 24 - Tuesday - Jesus as God

John 10:30 I and the Father are one.

Why could Jesus offer himself to the woman at the well as Living Water? And, why did the Jewish church leaders hate Jesus so much? They were constantly trying to test Him and make Him mess up. They saw how many people were following Him and wanted the crowds to see that Jesus was just a normal guy, not one to be revered and followed. Can you guess why?

Because Jesus claimed to be God. Can you imagine if you met someone who said he was God come in the flesh? You'd think he was crazy! The Pharisees didn't think Jesus was crazy. They thought he was trying to deceive the Jewish people and they didn't like it.

These are men that respected God so much that they weren't even allowed to say or write His full name! They felt it was too holy to be tarnished by them. So they were extra mad that Jesus claimed to be equal with God.

The difference between the Pharisees and us is that we know Jesus rose from the dead. The death and resurrection are history for us. It was the future for the Jewish leaders. Some people refer to it as "being on this side of the cross." Because we are on this side of the cross we can see that Jesus fulfilled all of the prophecies given throughout the Old Testament and is the Messiah.

Activity: Crack an egg and talk about how the shell, yolk, and white is all the egg, but there are three parts. Explain that God is three parts in one: The Father, the Son (Jesus) and the Holy Spirit.

Day 25 - Wednesday - The Helper

John 14:15, 16, 24-26 If you love me, you
will keep My commandments. And I will
ask the Father and He will give you
another Helper, that He may be with you
forever...He who does not love Me does
not keep My words; and the word which
you hear is not Mine, but the Father's who
sent Me. These things I have spoken to
you, while abiding with you. But the
Helper, the Holy Spirit, whom the Father
will send in My name, He will teach you
all things, and bring to your remembrance
all that I said to you.

There seems to be a real link between faith and obedience. Jesus says He knows we love Him if we obey His commandments. Notice that our love for God comes first and then the obedience. And how do we know His commandments? By reading the Bible. But He doesn't stop there. If you keep reading in the same passage, He tells the disciples He will send them a Helper called the Holy Spirit who will teach them and help them remember God's word. The Holy Spirit is also the one who helps us keep God's commandments. We can decide to keep them on our own, but will eventually fail. When we call on the Holy Spirit, He helps us keep God's commandments on a daily basis. Ask the Holy Spirit to help you each day.

Activity: Fill a laundry basket with a stack of books too heavy for one child to carry (with older children you might need to get creative). Have each child try to lift the basket. When they can't do it alone, offer to help them. Lift it together. Explain that keeping God's commandments on our own is impossible. The Holy Spirit helps us with our load and enables us to keep God's commandments.

Day 26 - Thursday - Obedience and Faith

> John 14:21 He who has My
> commandments and keeps them is the
> one who loves Me; and he who loves Me
> will be loved by My Father, and I will love
> him and will disclose Myself to him."

This verse brings up obedience first and then love. It's interesting because just a few verses beforehand in the passage start the opposite way. It's almost like "what came first, the chicken or the egg?" The love or the obedience? We are not saved through our good works but by the grace of God (Titus 3:5-7). But what if I told you we do in fact need to do something to be saved? The Bible talks about it in many verses (Romans 10:13 - Call on the name of Jesus and thou shall be saved; John 3:16 - ...whoever believes on Him shall be saved)

We must obey the call of God on our lives. Faith in and of itself is an act of obedience. When we obey the call of God, He reveals Himself to us and we come into relationship with Him. When we come into relationship with Him, we want to obey Him more so we obey His commandments. It becomes one big continuous cycle. Because believe me, obeying His call on your life is not the end of what God will ask of you. You may face many temptations or difficulties in life and you will need to obey God. If you do, He will reveal more and more of Himself to you and you will find yourself in a deeper relationship with Him.

Activity: Play the traditional trust game to show faith and obedience are related.

1. Have the child stand in front of you with his back to you.

2. On your command, have the child fall backward, trusting you will catch him.

3. Catch him!

Day 27 - Friday - What happens when we don't obey God?

Hebrews 3:13 But encourage one another day after day, as long as it is still called "Today," lest any one of you be hardened by the deceitfulness of sin.

Do you think that God has rules so that you won't have any fun in life? No! He has rules to protect you and because sinning keeps you from communing with God. HE is all good. He cannot be around sin, so when you sin and don't come before Him to ask for forgiveness it puts up a barrier in your relationship. He doesn't want that... He wants to be with you everyday. But sin hardens our heart. The more we disobey the farther from God we drift. Confessing our sins and obeying him is what brings us back into relationship with Him. If you feel yourself out on your own without the presence of God, it is likely you have neglected your relationship with Him, either through willful sin or through not spending enough time with Him. Confess this before Him and get back to a daily seeking of Him and His will for your life.

Activity: Salt dough hearts -Make a batch of salt dough. Roll it out flat and cut out hearts with cookie cutters. Let them dry into hardened hearts and paint them (optional). Talk about how sin makes our hearts hard.

Salt dough recipe: 1/2 cup salt, 1/2 cup water, 1 cup flour.

Directions:

1) Mix 1/2 cup salt and 1 cup flour.

2) Pour a little water in at a time and mix until dough forms. You may not need all the water. If you want to add food coloring - now is the time.

3) Roll dough out on a flat surface and cut out shapes.

4) To dry shapes, put them in the microwave for 1 minute. If they are still a little sticky, put them in the microwave for 20 second spurts until they are completely dry. (You should not smell burning. if you do burn them, you can incorporate that too by saying not only does sin harden our hearts, but sometimes we get burned!)

5) Let cool. If you didn't add food coloring, you can have kids paint them if you wish.

Alternately: you can bake shapes in a 325 degree (F) oven for 2-3 hours or until dry. Explain that sometimes sin is hardening our heart so slowly over time that we don't know it's happening until our hearts are already hard.

Day 28 - Fifth Saturday of Lent - Self Denial

Self-denial is the act of fasting or abstaining (not having any) of a particular thing. Jesus talks about fasting in terms of food in the New Testament. The hunger pains we feel are supposed to remind us that we depend on God for our very lives.

Some people combine fasting and prayer together when they are especially concerned about something or someone. They may fast for an entire day and pray throughout the day (especially at meal times when they would've been eating) for that person or situation. Others may fast one meal or a whole week. This practice is based on the account in Mark 9 when the disciples were unable to cast the demons out of a boy. They had cast out demons in the name of Jesus before and were confused why they couldn't this time. Jesus says to them in Mark 9:29, "This kind cannot come out by anything but prayer and fasting."

Self-denial in the Lenten tradition can take on many forms. It was originally meant as not eating meat on Ash Wednesday and Good Friday as a sign of solidarity with those who could and could not afford to buy meat (remembering the poor). As years passed, Fridays were added as a time to abstain from meat, and then the tradition started to include things like giving up vices (alcohol, desserts) and technology (television, internet, Facebook).

For our 40-day journey, the self-denial aspect is optional and should be made on a personal basis.

Activity: Eat beans and rice for one meal (or something else inexpensive like cereal). Take the difference in cost between your family's typical meal and the beans and rice and donate it to an organization that feeds those in poverty.

This could be your local food bank or homeless shelter or an international organization like World Vision or Feed the Children. As a family discuss what is being given so kids have an understanding of the self-denial aspect of the activity.

Fifth Sunday of Lent:

At lunch, talk about what you each learned in church this week. End with a family prayer - it doesn't have to be long... just a time to pray for the things you decided to focus on during the forty-day journey.

Day 29 - Monday - The Ten Commandments

Exodus 20: 1-17 Then God spoke all these words saying, "I am the Lord your God, who brought you out of the land of Egypt, out of the house of slavery (1) You shall have no other gods before Me. (2) You shall not make for yourself an idol, or any likeness of what is in heaven above or on the earth beneath or in the water under the earth. You shall not worship them or serve them; for I, the Lord your God, am a jealous God, visiting iniquity of the fathers on the children, on the third and fourth generations of those who hate Me, but showing loving-kindness to thousands, to those who love Me and keep My commandments. (3) You shall not take the name of the Lord your God in vain, for the Lord will not leave him unpunished who takes His name in vain. (4) Remember the Sabbath day to keep it holy. Six days you shall labor and do all your work, but the seventh day is a Sabbath of the Lord your God; in it you shall not do any work, you or your son or your daughter, your male or your female servant or your cattle or your sojourner who stays with you. For in six days the Lord made the heavens and the earth, the sea and all that is in them, and rested on the seventh day; therefore the Lord blessed the Sabbath day and made it holy. (5) Honor your father and your mother, that your days may be prolonged in the land which the Lord your God gives you. (6) You shall not murder. (7) You shall not commit adultery. (8) You shall not steal (9) You shall not bear false witness against your neighbor (10) You shall not covet your neighbor's house; you shall not covet your neighbor's wife or his male servant or his female servant or his ox or his donkey or anything that belongs to your neighbor. (numbers inserted by author for clarity)

We learned yesterday that if we love God, we keep His commandments. God gave many laws to the Jewish people: laws that had to do with what they could eat, who they could associate with, how to keep themselves and their community healthy and free of germs, and how to treat God and others. If our love for God is judged on if we obey Him, it's important to know what He expects of us. We focus on the Ten Commandments because of all the laws given to the Jews, they seem to be the only ones that Jesus focused on during his ministry.

Activity: Take some time to talk over the Ten Commandments and what they mean in practical terms.

Day 30 - Tuesday - The Greatest Commandment

Matthew 22:36-40 (someone asked him)
Teacher, which is the great
commandment in the Law?" And He said
to him, "You shall love the Lord your God
with all your heart, and with all your soul,
and with all your mind. This is the great
and foremost commandment. The second
is like it, You shall love your neighbor as
yourself. On these two commandments
depend the whole Law and the Prophets."

In many of Jesus' teachings and Paul's letters to early Christians, Jewish laws and customs are challenged. However, the basic Ten Commandments are never challenged. In fact, Jesus refers to them when asked what the greatest commandment is. Look at the 10 commandments from yesterday.... divide them into two groups. The first four deal with our relationship with God and the second six deal with our relationship with others. If we are focused on loving God with our whole being and loving our neighbors, we will automatically be obeying the Ten Commandments.

Activity: Draw or cut out a heart from a piece of paper. Talk about what ways we can love God with our whole hearts and our neighbors as ourselves. Write them on the heart.

Optional Reading: 1 Corinthians 13:4-8

Day 31 - Wednesday - GRACE!

John 8:3-11 And the scribes and the
Pharisees brought a woman caught in
adultery, and having set her in the midst
they said to Him, "Teacher, this woman
has been caught in adultery, in the very
act. Now in the Law Moses commanded us
to stone such women; what then do You
say?" And they were saying this, testing
Him, in order that they might have
grounds for accusing Him. But Jesus
stooped down, and with His finger wrote
on the ground. But when they persisted in
asking Him, He straightened up and said
to them, "He who is without sin among
you, let him be the first to throw a stone
at her." And again He stooped down, and
wrote on the ground. And when they
heard it, they began to go out one by one,
beginning with the older ones, and He
was left alone, and the woman, where she
was, in the midst. And straightening up,
Jesus said to her, "Woman, where are
they? Did no one condemn you?" And she
said, No one, Lord." And Jesus said,
"Neither do I condemn you; go your way.
From now on sin no more."

No one knows what Jesus wrote on the ground. What we
do know is that He did not want to stone the woman
for what the Jews considered a sin worthy of death. You
see, God is more interested in giving us grace than in
condemning us! Because His character is goodness we are
unable to be in His presence when sin is in our lives. He is

so interested in a relationship with us He sent His Son to pay the price for the sin in our lives. And once we come into a relationship with Him, He wants us to constantly be getting rid of that sin.

People get this confused. They wonder why there is such a focus on our sin. The reason is because God wants to get rid of the sin to get the important part - - spending life together. Walking with Him like Adam and Eve did in the garden. It all goes back to why we were created in the first place. God wants a relationship that doesn't rely on forced worship (like the angels). He wants a relationship with beings who choose to be with Him. Doesn't it feel so much better to have someone play with you because they want to and not because their mom makes them? That's how God feels when we choose to give up sin in our lives because we want to be with Him. And that's why He lets us choose Him instead of forcing us to believe in Him. Just like the boy on the playground who's chosen last for teams, God feels disappointed when mankind chooses sin over Him.

The story of Jesus and the gospel is really a love story. The one that God has for you! It isn't about our sin.... it's about the love of a good God who wants to be rid of that sin so He can get to you! It's all about YOU!

Activity: Make an Easter Garden

1. Get a large terracotta planter base and small terracotta planter from the hardware store.

2. Fill half the planter base with river rocks. Place the small pot on its side in the rocks.

3. Fill the other half of the planter base with potting soil making sure to cover the top of the small planter, leaving only the opening showing.

4. Sprinkle grass seed in the soil. Sprinkle a thin layer of soil over top the seeds.

5. Place your round-ish stone halfway over the small terracotta planter's opening.

6. Make 3 wooden crosses from twigs. (see Day 38 activity for instructions) and place behind the "tomb"

7. Mist soil daily. Grass should sprout within 7-10 days in time for Resurrection morning.

Day 32 - Thursday - Palm Sunday - The Triumphal Entry

Matthew 21:1-11 And when they had approached Jerusalem and had come to Bethphage, to the Mount of Olives, then Jesus sent two disciples, saying to them, "Go into the village opposite you, and immediately you will find a donkey tied there and a colt with her; untie them, and bring them to Me. And if anyone says something to you, you shall say, 'The Lord has need of them,' and immediately he will send them." ... and the disciples went and did just as Jesus had directed them, and brought the donkey and the colt, and laid on them their garments, on which He sat. And most the multitude spread their garments in the road, and others were cutting branches from the trees, and spreading them in the road. And the multitudes going before Him, and those who followed after were crying out, saying, "Hosanna to the Son of David; Blessed is He who comes in the name of the Lord; Hosanna in the highest!" And when He had entered Jerusalem, all the city was stirred, saying, "Who is this?" And the multitudes were saying, "This is the prophet Jesus, from Nazareth in Galilee."

Jesus was welcomed into the city by a crowd of people who believed Jesus would deliver them from the Roman Empire. They were looking for a leader who could help them in an uprising. With all the miracles He had performed and the large crowds that followed Him, Jesus was a good candidate.

Hosanna is a Jewish phrase of praise meaning "Save" or "Save us now." The crowd was looking for Jesus to 'save' them on earth. They had no idea in a week's time He would save them in the most important way possible - by His death on the cross.

Activity:

1) Tell the children you have a surprise for them.

2.) Hand each one an (empty) gift-wrapped box.

3.) When they open it, explain that the Jews thought Jesus was someone He was not, just as they thought the gift was something it was not. They misunderstood the reason for His coming. Imagine their disappointment when they realized He wasn't going to help them overthrow the Roman government.

Day 33 - Friday - The Last Supper

John 13: 1-5, 12-17, 20 Now before the Feast of the Passover, Jesus knowing that His hour had come that He should depart out of this world to the Father, having loved His own who were in the world, He loved them to the end. And during supper, the devil having already put into the heart of Judas Iscariot, the son of Simon, to betray Him, Jesus, knowing that the Father had given all things into His hands, and that He had come forth from God, and was going back to God, rose from supper, and laid aside His garments; and taking a towel, He girded Himself about. Then He poured water into the basin, and began to wash the disciples' feet, and to wipe them with the towel with which He was girded.

12. And so when He had washed their feet, and taken His garments, and reclined at the table again, He said to them, Do you know what I have done to you? You call Me Teacher and Lord; and you are right, for so I am. If I then, the Lord and the Teacher, washed your feet, you also ought to wash one another's feet. For I gave you an example that you also should do as I did to you. Truly, truly, I say to you, a slave is not greater than his master; neither is one who is sent greater than the one who sent him. If you know these things you are blessed if you do them.

20. Truly, truly, I say to you, he who
receives whomever I send receives Me;
and he who receives Me receives Him
who sent Me.

During the time of Jesus, the roads were dusty and everyone wore sandals. It was customary for people to rinse their feet upon entering a house. One of the last lessons Jesus teaches his followers is that we should be servants to each other. There is no one greater than the Master (Him) and He was a servant-leader. He didn't come to dominate the world, but to save it, and to save it through giving up his life. Most people think of power as something that allows you to make people do what you want, or to be able to get whatever you want in life because of who you are. Jesus shows us that true power is changing the world by loving others. When we look at history very few "powerful" people have changed the world for the better by living for their own pleasures and wants - the people who change the world are the ones who quietly sacrifice their own needs and comforts for the betterment of others.

Activity: Wash each other's feet. You will need a large washbasin or bowl, and several towels. You don't necessarily need soap. The activity is more for effect of how we are to be servant-leaders just like Christ. Pray silently for the person whose feet you are washing.... pray that their feet would follow in the footsteps of Jesus, that they would look to God to direct their path (Prov. 3:5-6), and that they would take the good news of the Gospel everywhere they go (Romans 10:14-15).

Day 34 - Sixth Saturday -

Complete the service project your family came up with several weeks ago.

Sixth Sunday- Palm Sunday;

At lunch, talk about what you each learned in church this week. End with a family prayer - it doesn't have to be long... just a time to pray for the things you decided to focus on during the forty-day journey.

Day 35 - Monday - The Bread and the Wine

Luke 22: 17-20 And when He had taken a cup and given thanks, He said, "Take this and share it among yourselves; for I say to you, I will not drink of the fruit of the vine from now on until the kingdom of God comes." And when He had taken some bread and given thanks, He broke it, and gave it to them saying, "This is My body which is given for you; do this in remembrance of Me." And in the same way He took the cup after they had eaten, saying, "This cup which is poured out for you is the new covenant in My blood."

I Corinthians 12: 26 For as often as you eat this bread and drink the cup, you proclaim the Lord's death until He comes.

The night before Jesus died, He and His disciples gathered together to celebrate the Jewish festival known as Passover. This was a week -long celebration commemorating how the lamb's blood saved the lives of the children of the Israelites the night before they left Egypt. Jesus takes the simple meal of Passover and makes it into a new symbol of His own body about to be broken. Christians today participate in something called Communion - a sacred (holy) act of remembering the death of Jesus through bread and wine. It's a somber act and to be taken seriously.

Activity:

Younger kids: Make and explain a traditional Jewish Seder plate - a small plate of specific food eaten before the Passover meal that holds deep significance to the Jewish people. (Directions on following page.)

Older kids who have expressed faith in Christ: Have communion together as a family, perhaps in the evening after supper, by candlelight. Consider reading I Corinthians 11: 23-34, which gives parameters around who should participate in communion and how.

Traditional Seder Plate:

There are six food items on the plate and then matzot crackers to the side on a napkin. Seder is the remembering of the plight of the Jews who were slaves in Egypt. It takes place during Passover when Jews remember the miracles of the Exodus - the redemption of God's people foreshadowing the Messiah to come.

1. The shankbone symbolized the lamb that was sacrificed the night before the Exodus and whose blood was spread on the doorframe. A roasted chicken neck is often substituted when lamb shankbone isn't available. This is symbolic only and is not consumed during the meal.

2. The hardboiled egg symbolizes the offerings brought by the Jews to the Old Testament Temple. It's removed from the plate and eaten during the Passover meal following observation of Seder.

3. Bitter herbs: The most common herbs used are Romaine or Endive lettuce leaves, or grated horseradish. This symbolizes the bitterness of slavery in Egypt for the Jews. The horseradish should be laid on a bed of Romaine and eaten together.

4. The mixture is made from peeled chopped apple, finely chopped walnuts, and a splash of wine. It symbolizes the brick and mortar made by the Jewish slaves in Egypt. The Mixture is placed in a piece of lettuce, put between two pieces of matzot and eaten.

5. The vegetable is a slice of onion or boiled potato. This symbolizes the hard labor done by the Jewish slaves. The Rabbi (or group leader) should dip it in salt water and give each person one bite.

6. A second bitter herb (lettuce) is typically Romaine and again symbolizes the bitterness of slavery. In addition to the piece under the horseradish, another piece appears on the plate and is dipped in salt water.

Day 36 - Tuesday - The Garden of Gethsemane

Matthew 26: 36,38-39, 42 Then Jesus came with them to a place called Gethsemane, and said to His disciples, "Sit here while I go over there and pray." (38) Then He went a little beyond them, and fell on His face and prayed, saying, "My Father, if it is possible, let this cup pass from Me, yet not as I will, but as Thou Wilt....." (42) He went away again a second time and prayed, saying, "My Father, if this cannot pass away unless I drink it, Thy will be done."

Jesus isn't only our example in leading others by serving them, but is also our example in obeying His Father. We see him vulnerable and anxious. The account in Mark 14:34 says He told Peter, James and John, "My soul is deeply grieved to the point of death; remain here and keep watch." He knows He's about to suffer a great deal physically and spiritually (all the sins of the world will be placed upon Him and He's beaten almost to death). It's something He'd rather not do, yet He submits to the Father and is obedient to the plan, knowing His death and resurrection is the only hope for mankind. How much more willing should we be to obey the will of God in our lives if Jesus was willing to die for us? John 15:13 says, "Greater love has no one than this, that one lay down his life for his friends." Jesus showed loved for his Father with His obedience and love for us by His death.

Activity: Play Simon Says or Mother May I to practice obedience.

Day 37 - Wednesday - Judas betrays Jesus

Matthew 26: 14-15 Then one of the twelve, named Judas Iscariot, went to the chief priests, and said, "What are you willing to give me to deliver Him up to you?" and they weighed out to him thirty pieces of silver. And from then on he began looking for a good opportunity to betray Him.

Mark 14: 43-46 And immediately while He was still speaking, Judas, one of the twelve, came up, accompanied by a multitude with swords and clubs, from the chief priests and the scribes and the elders. Now he who was betraying Him had given them a signal, saying, "Whomever I shall kiss, He is the one; seize Him, and lead Him away under guard." And after coming, He immediately went to Him, saying, "Rabbi!" and kissed Him. And they laid hands on Him, and seized Him.

In the time when Jesus lived, people greeted one another with a kiss on the cheek. Some cultures still do this today much like you may greet people you know well with a hug. Judas used the very symbol of friendship to betray Jesus.

Think of different ways we betray God with our actions. (examples: being mean to others, making fun of people, not letting others play with us, disobeying our parents or teachers, etc.) These very things are what put Jesus on the cross. He died for OUR sins. That should first make us feel sorry and then make us feel very thankful that Jesus is so willing to forgive us.

Activity: Have one child stand next to you. Give them a book and say one way we feel betrayed by friends. Add books one by one having each person in the group say a way they feel betrayed or how we mistreat one another. When the child starts to struggle with the load explain that Jesus was weighed down by our sins as He faced the cross AND He was at the same time betrayed by Judas and beaten by the soldiers. Explain that we, too, are sometimes weighed down by life's circumstances or the wrong things we do. With the help of Jesus, that load can be taken from us. Take the books from the child.

Day 38 - Holy Thursday - The Trial of Jesus

Mark 14:61-65 ... Again the high priest
was questioning Him, and saying to Him,
"Are You the Christ (Messiah), the Son of
the Blessed One?" And Jesus said, "I am;
and You shall see The son of man sitting
at the right hand of the Power, and
coming with the clouds of heaven." And
tearing his clothes, the high priest said,
"What further need do we have of
witnesses?" You have heard the
blasphemy; how does it seem to you?"
And they all condemned Him to be
deserving of death. And some began to
spit at Him, and to blindfold Him, and to
beat Him with their fists, and to say to
Him, "Prophesy!" and the officers
received Him with slaps in the face.

The Jewish leaders held a trial immediately - in the middle of the night! - to declare Jesus guilty of blasphemy. Blasphemy was punishable by death. They knew He claimed to be the Messiah and couldn't believe that He was. After questioning Him, they blindfolded and beat Him while mocking Him as a blasphemer.

In the early morning they brought Jesus to the Roman ruler Pilate asking that Jesus be put to death. They told Pilate that Jesus claimed to be King of the Jews - an affront to the Roman king. Pilate questioned Him and couldn't find that He had done anything wrong, but didn't want to make the Jewish leaders upset. So he brought Jesus and a brutal murderer name Barabbas before the gathered crowd of Jews and asked who they wanted him to release (he released one prisoner every Passover). The Jewish leaders mingled into the crowd and started chanting for Jesus to be crucified. The crowd took up the chant and Jesus was condemned to die.

The Roman soldiers took Jesus into custody. They beat Him and taunted Him as the King of the Jews. They plucked out His beard, put a crown of thorns on His head and beat Him almost until He was dead with a whip. He was barely able to walk when He was forced to carry His own cross up the road to the place where they crucified people. In fact, a man - Simon of Cyrene - was pulled from the crowd to carry the cross since Jesus was so weak. (Mark 15:1-21)

Activity: Make a small wooden cross. Place the cross in a prominent place in your home. Every time you see it today, thank Jesus for going to the cross in your place.

1. Take two small sticks (or twigs from a bush) and hot glue them together into the shape of a cross.

2. Take a piece of twine and wrap it around in a crisscross pattern over the intersection. Put a dot of glue on the back to keep the twine in place. TIP: My twine was pretty thick. I took one strand out of the combination of strands that make up the twine to use for this project.

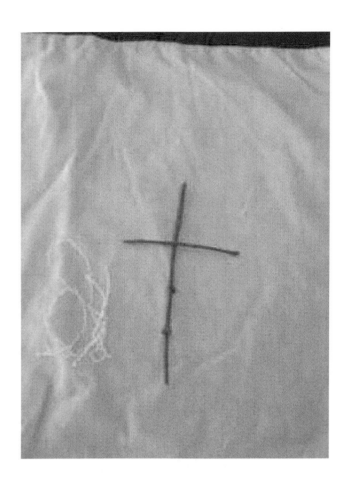

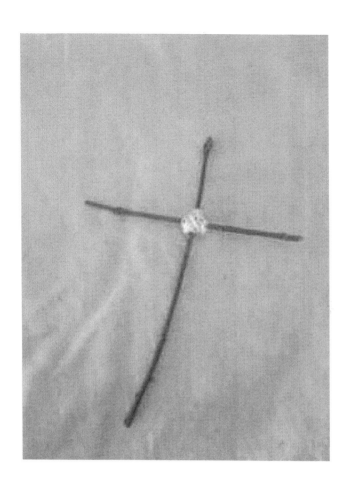

Day 39 - Good Friday - Crucifixion, Death and Burial of Jesus

> Mark 15:22 - And they brought Him to the place Golgotha, which is translated, Place of a Skull. And they tried to give Him wine mixed with myrrh; but He did not take it. And they crucified Him, and divided up His garments among themselves, casting lots for them to decide what each should take.

Whew! So many things happened on Friday because the Jewish leaders were trying to fit everything in before the start of the Sabbath on Friday at sundown. They worked from sundown on Thursday (so technically their Friday since their days go from sundown to sundown) until sundown on Friday to get everything done. They didn't want the Sabbath to come and go and perhaps, have Jesus be let go, or worse yet, escape with the help of his followers. They had to get it done and they had to get it done NOW!

After Jesus is severely beaten and barely able to make it to the place of crucifixion (Golgotha - "The Place of the Skull") He is nailed to a large beam of wood and placed on a cross. He is hung between two thieves, in the place where Barabbas the murderer should have hung. Late in the afternoon His spirit passes from His body and He dies.

The sky became dark. There was an earthquake so strong that rocks split in two and the gravestones in cemeteries broke. (Mark 15:33, Matthew 27:50-51) All of creation groaned in agony. The King of kings and the Lord of lords was dead. To the disciples and the world, it seemed as if Jesus was defeated and with it their dreams.

Activity: There is no fun activity today. Today is the most somber of the whole of the Easter season. It is a day of mourning. Jesus is dead. His mother and followers are in a state of despair and confusion. Take a moment to sit in that feeling. Some churches have a service today to observe the solemnity of Good (Holy) Friday. Consider singing a few hymns together as a family about Jesus' time on the cross. Two good ones are *The Old Rugged Cross* and *There is a Fountain*. If you have any candles burning in the house, put them out as a sign of the death of a loved one.

The Old Rugged Cross

Rev. G. B.

Rev. Geo. Bennard

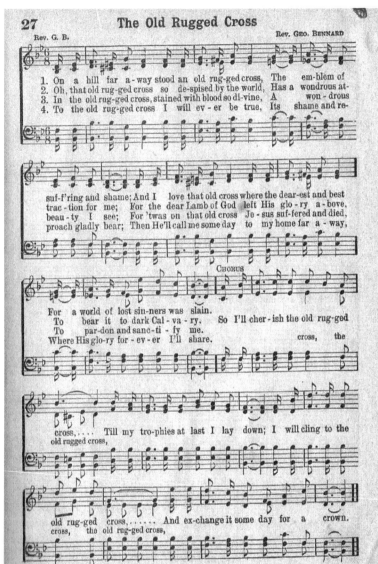

1. On a hill far a-way stood an old rug-ged cross, The em-blem of
2. Oh, that old rug-ged cross so de-spised by the world, Has a wondrous at-
3. In the old rug-ged cross, stained with blood so di-vine, A won-drous
4. To the old rug-ged cross I will ev-er be true, Its shame and re-

suf-f'ring and shame; And I love that old cross where the dear-est and best
trac-tion for me; For the dear Lamb of God left His glo-ry a-bove,
beau-ty I see; For 'twas on that old cross Je-sus suf-fered and died,
proach gladly bear; Then He'll call me some day to my home far a-way,

CHORUS

For a world of lost sin-ners was slain. So I'll cher-ish the old rug-ged
To bear it to dark Cal-va-ry.
To par-don and sanc-ti-fy me.
Where His glo-ry for-ev-er I'll share. cross, the

cross,.... Till my tro-phies at last I lay down; I will cling to the
old rugged cross,

old rug-ged cross,...... And ex-change it some day for a crown.
cross, the old rug-ged cross,

Day 40 - Saturday - Easter Eve

Can you imagine how the followers of Jesus felt the day after His crucifixion? Here was the beloved teacher they followed - some of them for three years - who they saw heal the sick, raise the dead, and cast out demons. The man they thought would rescue them from the Roman Empire. Now what would they do? Would the Romans come after them too?

Reflect on what it would mean to be unsure of your future. Thank God for loving us enough to send His Son to die for us.

Activity:

Make resurrection cookies - fun for all ages!

Recipe: (owner unknown, I got it from nivadivup.blogspot.com)

First preheat the oven to 300 degrees.

Ingredients:

1 c. whole pecans

1 tsp vinegar

3 egg whites

1 pinch of salt

1 c. of sugar

You will need:

Mixing bowl, wooden spoon, Bible, Ziplock baggie, wax paper, cookie sheet, tape, mixer

Place pecans in the baggie and let the children beat them with the wooden spoon to break into small pieces. Explain that after Jesus was arrested, He was beaten by the Roman soldiers. (Read John 19: 1-3)

Let the children smell the vinegar. Put 1 tsp. into a mixing bowl. Explain that when Jesus was thirsty on the cross, He was given vinegar to drink. (Read John 19: 28-30)

Add the egg whites to the vinegar. Eggs represent life. Explain that Jesus gave his life for us. (Read John 10: 10-11)

Sprinkle a little salt into the children's hand and let them taste it, then brush the rest into the bowl. Explain that it represents the salty tears shed by Jesus' followers and the bitterness of our own sin. (Read Luke 23:27)

Add 1 cup of sugar. Explain that the sweetest part of this story is that Jesus died because He loves us. He wants us to know and belong to Him. (Read Psalm 34:8 and John 3:16)

Beat with mixer on high speed for 11-15 minutes until stiff peaks form. Explain that the color white represents the purity in God's eyes of those whose sins have been cleansed by Jesus. (Read Isaiah 1:18 and John 3:1-3)

Fold in broken nuts. Drop by teaspoon onto wax paper-covered cookie sheet. Explain that each mound represents the rocky tomb where Jesus' body was laid. (Read Matthew 27: 65-66)

Put cookie sheet in oven. Close the door and turn the oven OFF. Give the child a piece of tape and seal the door. Explain that Jesus' tomb was sealed. (Read Matthew 27:65-66)

Explain they may feel sad to leave the cookies in the oven

overnight. Jesus' followers were in despair when the tomb was sealed. (Read John 16:20 and 22)

Go to bed!

Sunday - EASTER MORNING!

On Resurrection morning, open the oven and give everyone a cookie! Notice the cracked surface and take a bite. The cookies are hollow! On the first Resurrection Day, Jesus' followers were amazed to find the tomb open and empty. (Read Matthew 28: 1-9)

He has risen! Hallelujah!

Celebrate as a family by going to church to worship the ONE who gave His life for you and rose so that you might live eternally with Him. Spend the afternoon in JOY experiencing the freedom we have in Christ. If you are doing an Easter egg hunt, tell the kids the eggs are like the gospel, when you open them up there's a free gift!

I hope you and your family enjoyed this 40-day journey. It was so sweet a time for our family I don't want it to end. The great thing is it doesn't have to. Continue teaching your children about the good news of the gospel. There are many great resources out there. And most of all, don't forget how much Jesus loves YOU!

About the Author

Leighann Marquiss is the author of *Showing Heart: The story of how one boy defied the odds*, a memoir chronicling her family's journey through the ups and downs of having a child with a congenital heart defect. Reading much like a novel, *Showing Heart* will make you laugh, cry, and appreciate the joy in your own life. She is also the author of You Are Not Alone: An Insider's Guide to Facing Prenatal Diagnosis. Leighann lives with her husband, Henry, and four children in Western Pennsylvania. She writes regularly at www.leighannmarquiss.com

33211541R00059

Made in the USA
Lexington, KY
09 March 2019